Rookie reader®

 SO-BCO-665

Pickles in My Soup

Written by
Mary Pearson

Illustrated by
Tom Payne

Children's Press®
A Division of Grolier Publishing
New York • London • Hong Kong • Sydney
Danbury, Connecticut

To Karen and Jessica, my favorite pickle-eaters
—M. P.

Reading Consultants
Linda Cornwell
Coordinator of School Quality and Professional Improvement
(Indiana State Teachers Association)

Katharine A. Kane
Education Consultant
(Retired, San Diego County Office of Education
and San Diego State University)

Visit Children's Press® on the Internet at:
http://publishing.grolier.com

Library of Congress Cataloging-in-Publication Data
Pearson, Mary (Mary E.)
    Pickles in my soup / written by Mary Pearson: illustrated by Tom Payne
    p. cm. -- (Rookie reader)
    Summary: A girl loves to eat pickles in all kinds of unusual combinations.
    ISBN 0-516-21636-8 (lib.bdg.)   0-516-26550-4(pbk.)
    [1. Pickles Fiction. 2. Stories in rhyme.] I. Payne, Thomas, ill. II. Title. III. Serie
PZ8.3.P27472Pi 1999
[E]--dc21   99-22470
                                                                        CIP
                                                                        AC

Pickles! Pickles!
I love pickles.

They are all I want to eat.

CRUNCH
CRUNCH
CRUNCH
CRUNCH

PICKLES

I slice them on my cereal.

I slap them on my meat.

Pickles in spaghetti,

pickles all alone,

pickles in my pudding,

and on my ice cream cone.

Pickles topped with onions,

pickles with baloney,

oh, and I really love
pickles in macaroni.

Pickles dipped in chocolate,

pickles rolled in flakes,

pickles on my pizza,

pickles on pancakes!

Pickles in my soup,

pickles on my cake.

Stop! No more pickles, please!
I have a tummy ache!

WORD LIST (47 WORDS)

a	dipped	no	slice
ache	eat	oh	soup
all	flakes	on	spaghetti
alone	have	onions	stop
and	I	pancakes	them
are	ice	pickles	they
baloney	in	pizza	to
cake	love	please	topped
cereal	macaroni	pudding	tummy
chocolate	meat	really	want
cone	more	rolled	with
cream	my	slap	

ABOUT THE AUTHOR

Mary Pearson has been writing stories, either in her head or on paper, since she was eight years old. When she became a teacher, she loved writing with her students, and they provided her with lots of ideas for new stories. Now she writes full time from her home in San Diego, California, where she lives with her husband, two daughters, golden retriever, floppy-eared bunny, and a few critters who weren't invited but showed up anyway. Of course, she loves pickles!

ABOUT THE ILLUSTRATOR

Thomas Payne has been a humorous illustrator for a very long time. His work has appeared in all sorts of books and magazines. He commutes into his studio, which he shares with some other "arty" people in Albany, New York, from his home in the nearby Helderberg Mountains. He lives with his wife, Anne, and his son, Thomas.